HURRICANES

HURRICANES

SALLY LEE

Franklin Watts
New York/Chicago/London/Sydney
A First Book

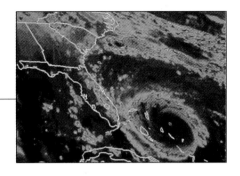

Photographs copyright ©:
Weatherstock, cover, 31 (top & bottom); NOAA, 1; AP/Wide World, 6, 32 (bottom),
33 (top), 37, 47, 48, 54; Jules Bucher/Photo Researchers, 10; Dr. Fred Espenak,
SPL/Photo Researchers, 12; The Rosenberg Library, Galveston, Texas, 28; Fred
Whitehead,/Earth Scenes, 32 (top); Orlando Sentinel/Gamma-Liaison, 33 (bottom);
Sygma, 34; D. Aubert/Sygma, 35; Ray Pfortner/Peter Arnold, Inc., 36;
Reuters/Bettmann, 39; Bruno P. Zehnder/Peter Arnold, Inc., 43;
UPI/Bettmann, 44.

Library of Congress Cataloging-in-Publication Data

Lee, Sally.
Hurricanes / by Sally Lee.
p.   cm.—(A First book)
Includes bibliographical references and index.
Summary: A discussion of hurricanes, their formation and
structure, forecasting, and safety. Includes some related science
projects.
ISBN 0-531-20152-X   (HC : library binding)
0-531-15665-6 (paperback)
1. Hurricanes—Juvenile literature. [1. Hurricanes.] I. Title.
II. Series.
QC944.L44 1993
551.55'2—dc20
92-27367 CIP AC

CONTENTS

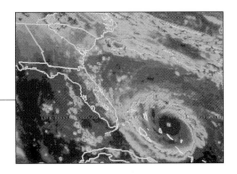

INTRODUCTION

WHAT IS A HURRICANE?

In August 1992, residents throughout southern Florida waited in fear of Andrew, the monstrous storm from the sea. His satellite picture looked terrifying, a compact, powerful swirl of clouds. Andrew had already killed four people in the Bahamas. As he approached Florida, thousands of people evacuated their homes in Miami, Miami Beach, and other communities that lay in the path of the huge storm. At the last minute, Andrew turned slightly south, sparing Miami, but with winds peaking at 164 mph (264 kph), the storm cut a swath of devastation through heavily populated towns in South Dade County. Andrew moved west across Florida and regained strength over the Gulf of Mexico. He then turned north and bore down on southeastern Louisiana, where several more towns were severely damaged and more than 44,000 were left homeless.

In Florida, an incredible 63,000 homes were destroyed, and the Homestead Air Force Base was decimated. Thirty-three deaths were attributed to Andrew, as well as an astounding $30 billion in damage, making this the most expensive natural disaster to ever hit the United States.

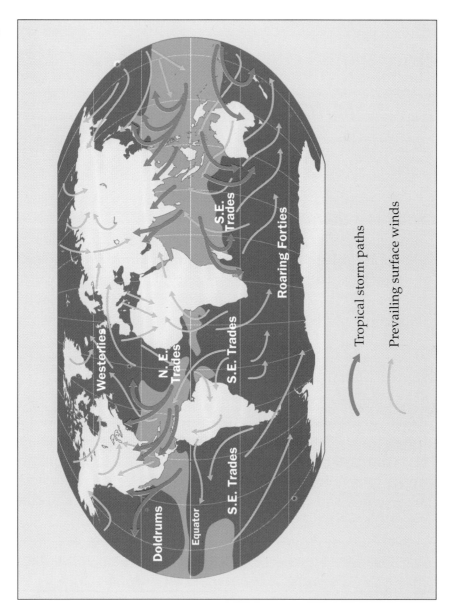

Map of prevailing winds.

A hurricane is a powerful, whirling storm with strong winds whipping around a relatively calm center. Although the wind must reach speeds of 74 mph (118 kmph) to be classified as a hurricane, speeds of 100–150 mph (193–240 kmph) or more are common. In rare instances, wind speed may reach 200 mph (321 kmph).

Hurricanes are born over the warm tropical oceans near the equator. Starting as small areas of thunderstorms, they can grow in size and strength until they measure 200–500 miles (320–804 km) across. The whole storm moves forward, and because they last for several days or even weeks, they cause more destruction than any other type of storm on earth.

In spite of their destructive nature, hurricanes have some benefits. They bring needed rain to many regions of the world, including parts of the United States. They are also important to the world's heat transfer system. Hurricanes move heat and energy from the equator to cooler areas toward the poles.

Hurricane winds, like all other winds, are caused by differences in atmospheric (air) pressure. Atmospheric pressure is the weight of air pushing down on the earth. In areas of high pressure, the weather is generally clear. Low pressure areas generally have wet and stormy weather. When the pressure gets very low, serious storms such as hurricanes occur.

Just as water flows downhill, air flows from areas of high pressure to areas of low pressure. This flow of air (wind) is fastest when there is a large difference in pressure between neighboring areas. The extremely low pressure of a hurricane causes a large difference in the pressure between

Barometers are used to measure atmospheric (air) pressure, which is important in forecasting weather and determining the severity of tropical storms and hurricanes.

the storm and the surrounding area. Air rushing into this low pressure area accounts for the hurricane's intense winds.

Because air pressure is measured with a barometer, it is often called *barometric pressure.* Two types of barometers are used by scientists to determine air pressure. In a *mercury barometer,* pressure from the surrounding air pushes down on a small amount of mercury in a container and forces some of the mercury up a tube. The height of mercury in the tube is measured in inches, millimeters, or millibars. (A bar is a unit of pressure in the metric system that is equal to 29.53 inches of mercury. It takes 1,000 millibars to make a bar.)

An *aneroid barometer* measures the pressure of the air pressing against a metal chamber from which part of the air has been removed. As the chamber expands and contracts, a dial indicates the air pressure.

The average barometric pressure at sea level over the Earth is 29.92 inches of mercury (1,013 millibars). In hurricanes, however, it is considerably lower. Hurricane Gilbert holds the record for the lowest pressure ever recorded in the Western Hemisphere; on September 14, 1988, his pressure dropped to 26.13 inches (855 millibars).

WHERE HURRICANE GETS ITS NAME
The word hurricane comes from the Spanish word huracan, meaning "great wind," or from similar words used by Caribbean Indian tribes to describe evil spirits, storm gods, and big winds.

Different parts of the world have different names for these massive storms. They are called cyclones in the Indian Ocean and near Australia, and typhoons in the western Pacific. In the rest of the Pacific Ocean, the Atlantic Ocean, the Caribbean, and the Gulf of Mexico they are called hurricanes. Similar storms in Australia are called willy-willies.

FAMOUS HURRICANES
Some hurricanes have become famous for the amount of death and damage they have caused. On September 8, 1900, a hurricane battered the island of Galveston, off the

A color enhanced satellite image of Hurricane Hugo shows the intensity of wind and rain in various parts of the storm.

Texas coast. The city was devastated by high winds and a 15-foot (5-meter) surge of water that swept over the island. More than 6,000 people were killed. It was one of the worst natural disasters ever to hit the United States.

Another deadly hurricane hit Lake Okeechobee, Florida, in 1928. When the hurricane wind and waves broke an earthen dike, Lake Okeechobee emptied onto the flat farmland. In just a few hours, 1,836 people downed and another 1,849 were injured.

Until Andrew in 1992, Hurricane Hugo was the United States' most expensive storm. During his violent visit he caused an estimated $7 billion in damage in the United States and another $3 billion in the Caribbean.

Death tolls from storms in the Western Hemisphere can't compare with those on the other side of the Earth. An estimated 300,000 lives were lost in 1881 when a typhoon hit the Haifong area of China. Some of the world's most disastrous storms occur along the densely populated areas of the Bay of Bengal. On October 7, 1737, a tropical cyclone hit Calcutta, India, killing more than 300,000 people. A similar storm in 1876 killed an estimated 100,000 people near the Bay of Bengal. When many of the dead were not promptly removed, several deadly diseases were spawned, eventually taking 100,000 more lives.

Death tolls have been even higher in modern times. The deadliest cyclone on record occurred in Bangladesh in 1970. Experts at the United Nations estimated the death toll to be greater than 500,000 from the storm itself and the diseases it caused. Another 100,000 residents of this tiny country were killed by a cyclone in 1991.

HURRICANE FACT SHEET

- A hurricane is a large whirling storm that normally measures 200 to 500 miles (320 to 800 km) across.
- On the average, six Atlantic hurricanes occur per year.
- A typical hurricane has sustained winds of 100–150 mph (160–240 kmph). Winds in some stronger storms may exceed 200 mph (320 kmph).
- The eye of a hurricane averages 14–25 miles (22–40 km) across. Large storms may have eyes up to 50 miles (80 km) across. The eye is relatively calm compared to the winds in the eye wall.
- The winds of a hurricane spin counterclockwise in the Northern Hemisphere and clockwise in the Southern Hemisphere.
- The hurricane season in the North Atlantic is June 1 to November 30. In the Southern Hemisphere the season is from November to June. Over the Western Pacific, the tropical cyclone season is never quite over.
- If the heat released by an average hurricane in one day could be converted to electricity, it could supply the United States' electrical needs for about six months.
- The heat energy released by a hurricane in one day can equal the energy released by the fusion of four hundred 20-megaton hydrogen bombs.
- As it travels across the ocean, a hurricane can pick up as much as two billion tons of water a day through evaporation and sea spray.
- Each second, some 2 million metric tons of air are circulated in, up, and out of the hurricane.

1

THE BIRTH OF A MONSTER

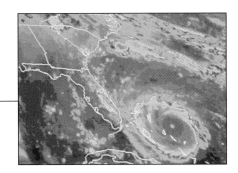

SETTING THE STAGE

It is summer in the Northern Hemisphere. The sun, directly overhead, provides greater amounts of energy north of the equator. The sun's heat evaporates large amounts of water and warms the surface of the tropical oceans to more than 80° F (27° C). Water this warm is necessary for the formation of hurricanes.

Into this hot humid area drifts a region of low pressure called a *tropical wave*. A typical wave contains an unorganized mass of showers and thunderstorms. As the wave drifts over the tropical ocean it draws in warm, moist tropical air. The air rises and cools. Much of its water vapor condenses into water droplets which form clouds.

When water vapor condenses from a gas to a liquid, heat is given off. This heat rises and triggers strong updrafts that pull warm moist air even higher.

FROM DISTURBANCE TO HURRICANE

The continuous growth of storm clouds results in a large area of thunderstorms that may last more than a day. This is called a *tropical disturbance*. These disturbances are

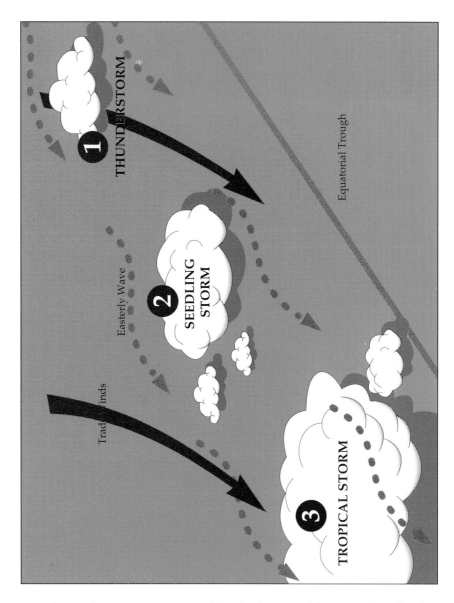

THUNDERSTORM 1

SEEDLING STORM 2

TROPICAL STORM 3

Easterly Wave

Trade Winds

Equatorial Trough

Areas of low pressure called tropical waves drift across the tropics causing showers and thunderstorms. If conditions are right, some of these waves may escalate into tropical storms and hurricanes.

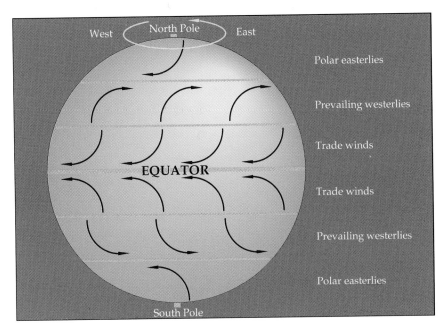

West · North Pole · East

Polar easterlies

Prevailing westerlies

Trade winds

EQUATOR

Trade winds

Prevailing westerlies

Polar easterlies

South Pole

When the wind in a tropical storm reaches the speed of 74 mph (119 kmph) the storm officially becomes a hurricane.

quite common in the tropics.

Air from a broad area surrounding the disturbance begins to flow inward toward the low-pressure center. The movement of air is given a twist by the *Coriolis force.* This force is a result of the Earth's rotation. It causes winds in low pressure systems to curve counterclockwise in the Northern Hemisphere and clockwise in the Southern Hemisphere.

When the winds begin to circle around a poorly defined center, the storm is called a *tropical depression.* It contains thunderstorms and wind speeds less than 38 mph (61 kmph). A depression becomes a *tropical storm* when its

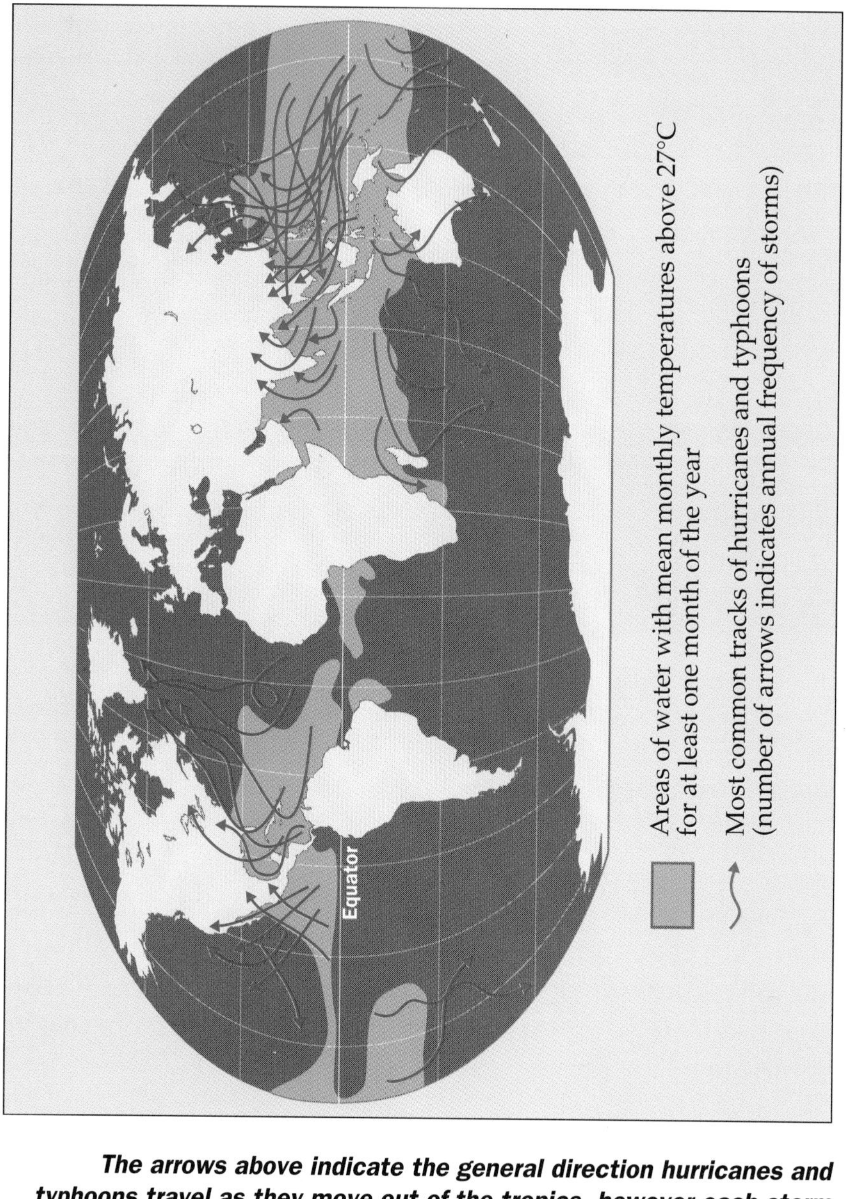
Equator
Areas of water with mean monthly temperatures above 27°C for at least one month of the year
Most common tracks of hurricanes and typhoons (number of arrows indicates annual frequency of storms)

The arrows above indicate the general direction hurricanes and typhoons travel as they move out of the tropics, however each storm has its own unique path which is difficult to predict.

winds reach 39 mph (63 kmph). At this point meteorologists give it a name and watch it even more closely. Under the right conditions, the pressure continues to drop. The storm tightens and the winds increase to more than 74 mph (119 kmph). Now the storm has officially become a hurricane (or cyclone or typhoon depending on the storm's location).

GETTING STRONGER

About a hundred easterly waves travel across the tropics during the North Atlantic hurricane season, but only a few become tropical storms. Fewer still reach hurricane strength. Scientists are still not sure exactly why some depressions fizzle out while others turn into violent hurricanes.

One necessary ingredient in the strengthening of a storm is an upper level high pressure system with light winds above it. These winds remove air rising out of the top of the storm. By eliminating the air at the top, more air is drawn in at the bottom. The rapidly rising air reduces the air pressure at the surface and intensifies the storm.

While light winds at the top of a storm encourage its growth, strong horizontal winds have the opposite effect. Strong winds blowing across the storm at various levels of the atmosphere shear off the clouds instead of allowing them to build straight up to high levels. This weakens the developing storm and prevents it from reaching hurricane strength.

BIRTH PLACES OF HURRICANES

Most hurricanes form in two general bands 5° to 30° latitude north and south of the equator. Hurricanes cannot form closer to the equator than 5° because here the Coriolis force is too weak to provide the necessary spin to the storm. Hurricanes also rarely form further than 30° north or south of the equator. Past that point, the stronger westerly winds in the upper levels of the atmosphere destroy developing hurricanes.

In the North Atlantic, hurricane season extends from June 1 to November 30, with most storms coming during August, September, and October. Storms in the Southern Hemisphere form during their summer and autumn seasons, November through June.

SAFFIR-SIMPSON SCALE

Hurricanes are classified by the Saffir-Simpson scale. It considers such things as barometric pressure, wind speed and storm surge. The scale ranks hurricanes from 1 to 5. Categories 4 and 5 are the most serious storms. Category 5 storms are rare and unforgettable. When Hurricane Gilbert crossed Cozumel, Mexico in 1988 he was a 5. That was the first category 5 storm in the Western Hemisphere since Camille hit the Louisiana-Mississippi border in 1969. Hurricane Andrew in 1992 was the latest.

NAMING HURRICANES

Once a disturbance becomes a tropical storm, it is given a name. This gives meteorologists an easy way to refer to it as they track the storm's progress.

Long ago, West Indian hurricanes were named after the particular saint's day on which they occurred. Later, hurricanes were identified by their latitude and longitude. This system was confusing, especially when more than one

THE SAFFIR-SIMPSON SCALE

Category	Barometric Pressure	Wind (mph)	Potential Damage
1	Over 28.94 inches	74 – 95	Trees, bushes, and unanchored mobile homes are damaged.
2	28.50 – 28.91	96 – 100	Trees are blown over. Exposed mobile homes are heavily damaged. Minor damage to house roofs.
3	27.91 – 28.47	111 – 130	Leaves are stripped from trees; large trees are uprooted. Mobile homes are destroyed. Some structural damage to buildings.
4	27.17 – 27.88	131 – 155	Street signs are blown down. Damage to windows, doors, roofs. Flooding inland as far as six miles. Buildings near shore maintain heavy damage.
5	Less than 27.17	Greater than 155	Heavy damage to windows, doors, roofs. Small buildings completely destroyed. Major damage to structures less than 15 feet above sea level within 500 yards of shore.

SCHEDULE OF NAMES FOR ATLANTIC STORMS

1993	1994	1995	1996
Arlene	Alberto	Alison	Arthur
Bret	Beryl	Barry	Bertha
Cindy	Chris	Chantal	Cesar
Dennis	Debby	Dean	Dolly
Emily	Ernesto	Erin	Edouard
Floyd	Florence	Felix	Fran
Gert	Gordon	Gabriell	Gustav
Harvey	Helene	Humberto	Hortense
Irene	Isaac	Iris	Isidore
Jose	Joyce	Jerry	Josephine
Katrina	Keith	Karen	Klaus
Lenny	Leslie	Luis	Lili
Maria	Michael	Marilyn	Marco
Nate	Nadine	Noel	Nana
Ophelia	Oscar	Opal	Omar
Philippe	Patty	Pablo	Paloma
Rita	Rafael	Roxanne	Rene
Stan	Sandy	Sebastien	Sally
Tammy	Tony	Tanya	Teddy
Vince	Valerie	Van	Vicky
Wilma	William	Wendy	Wilfred

storm was in the area at one time.

In 1953 the U.S. Weather Bureau officially started naming hurricanes after women. The names were easy to pronounce, easy to remember, and were less likely to cause confusion than other methods. In the late 1970s men's names, as well as Hawaiian and Spanish names, were added. Now alphabetical lists alternating male and female names are used.

There are separate sets of names for hurricanes in the North Atlantic and for typhoons in the Pacific. The lists of names for North Atlantic hurricanes are repeated every six years. If a hurricane has been especially deadly or damaging, its name is removed from the list.

2

THE STRUCTURE OF A HURRICANE

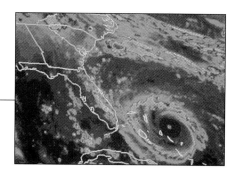

A hurricane is a giant heat engine. Every second in a hurricane's life, about two million tons of warm air shoot up through the eye wall. As the moisture in the warm air condenses to form clouds, heat energy is given off to drive the winds of the storm.

A hurricane is like a giant top that spins rapidly while it moves slowly across the floor. Pushed along by the easterly trade winds, a developing storm generally travels toward the west or northwest at speeds between 10 and 20 mph (16–32 kmph). As it strengthens and swings away from the tropics, it may speed up to 20 or 30 mph (32–48 kmph). But hurricane movements are unpredictable. They may speed up, slow down, or even stop for a while to build up strength. Some seem to creep across the ocean while a few have raced forward at more than 50 mph (80 kmph).

PARTS OF A HURRICANE

Eye. In the midst of violently whirling winds is an area of relative calm called the eye. Here winds are lighter and skies are clear or partly cloudy. It is the warmest part of the hurricane and has the lowest air pressure. The eye averages

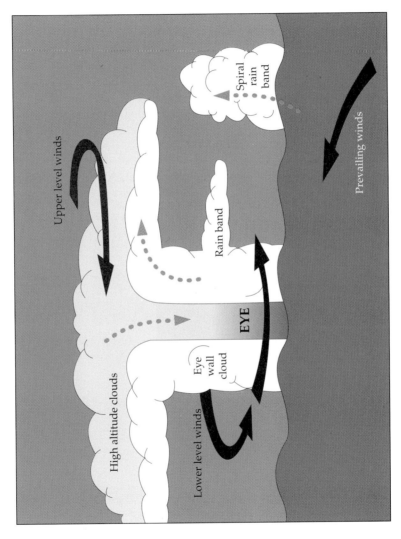

*A hurricane consists of strong wind and rain clouds spiraling
around a low pressure center called the eye.*

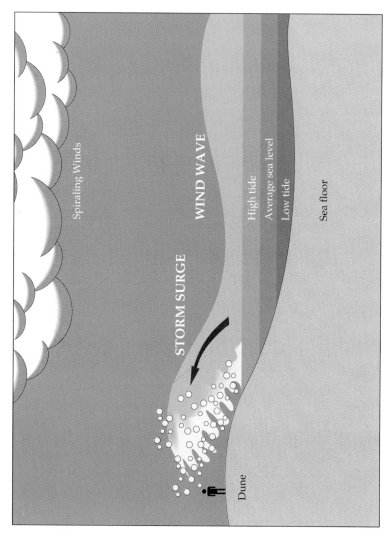

As a hurricane makes landfall it brings ashore a mound of water that can raise the mean (average) sea level by as much as 10 to 20 feet (3 to 6 m). This storm surge and its accompanying wind waves make a destructive and often deadly combination.

15 miles (24 km) across. Larger storms, such as typhoons in the Pacific, may have eyes as wide as 50 miles (80 km).

The eye can be dangerous. Those who think it is safe to venture out into this calmer area may be hit suddenly by the violent winds on the back side of the storm.

Eye Wall. Surrounding the eye is the eye wall, a more or less solid bank of thunderstorms 5 to 30 miles (8 to 48 km) wide. The eye wall contains the most damaging winds and produces the heaviest rain of the storm.

Rainbands. Also part of this large circulating storm are a series of dense clouds called *rainbands.* These long strips of clouds spiral in toward the center of the storm. It is the rainbands that give hurricanes their pinwheel appearance on satellite photos. The outer edges of the rainbands may reach the shore several hundred miles ahead of the eye itself. Their heavy rain can cause severe flooding.

Outflow shield. As the warm moist air rises rapidly through the storm, it eventually reaches the top. The air spirals out of the top and is carried away by high altitude winds. This outflowing air creates a canopy of clouds, called the outflow shield.

STORM SURGES

Most people think the most dangerous element in a hurricane is its violent wind, but this is not true. Most deaths and damage are caused by the storm surge that is blamed for nine out of every ten hurricane deaths.

Like a giant straw, the low pressure in the center of the

A hurricane's high wind and 15-foot (5-m) storm surge killed more than 6,000 people and devastated the city of Galveston, Texas, in 1900.

hurricane sucks up a mound of water about a foot (.3 meter) high and 50 miles (80 km) wide. As the center of the hurricane moves over land, this mound of high water is carried a short distance inland. The surge can raise the mean (average) level of the sea by as much as 20 feet (6 m). This sudden rise in sea level pushes water further onto the shore and can cause serious flooding to oceanfront property. The surge can be even more serious if it comes at the same time as a normal high tide.

The storm surge is not a giant wave as some people think. It is a sudden rise in the water level. It comes at a time when many areas are already flooded by torrential rain, so the results can be devastating. Most of the 6,000 deaths in the Galveston hurricane in 1900 were blamed on the surge that raised the water level by 4 feet (1.2 m) in only four seconds.

A surge is dangerous enough when it rushes upon a flat coastal area. It is even more devastating when it is forced into a narrow channel, such as a bay or the mouth of a river. The rushing water is squeezed together and can form a racing wall of water capable of destroying everything in its path.

To add to the potential destruction by water, the surge is topped by large breaking waves that have been whipped up by the wind. These powerful waves smash structures not designed to withstand their force. They can sweep away people, animals, and anything else in their way. The water erodes beaches and coastal highways, and can weaken the foundations of buildings and bridges.

3

WHEN A HURRICANE HITS LAND

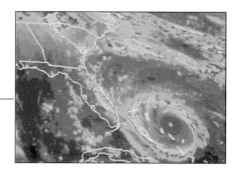

WARNING SIGNS

Even before a hurricane can be seen, there is a noticeable difference in the sea. The storm may still be 500 miles (800 km) away when the long, slow waves pushed ahead of the storm begin pounding heavily on the shore. These waves break at a much slower rate than normal.

As the storm approaches, high, feathery cirrus clouds appear in the clear sky. They often seem to radiate from a central point on the horizon. Later, the body of the storm comes into view, looking like a mass of clouds the color of dirty snow. Low, swift moving clouds move from left to right across the sky.

While the center of the storm is still 100 miles (160 km) or more away, rainbands may begin crossing the shoreline. Each band brings with it torrential rain and strong wind. The wind and rain increase as the bands closer to the storm center arrive.

Finally the full force of the hurricane hits. For two to four hours, winds roaring at more than 75 mph (120 kph) uproot trees, rip roofs off houses, and shatter windows. Sheets of rain pouring from the sky blow sideways through

(Top) An approaching hurricane is seen as a mass of clouds creeping over the horizon. (Bottom) Hurricane winds whip up huge waves 5 to 10 feet (1.5 to 3 m) high. These waves are especially dangerous when combined with the storm surge.

(Top) Trees in South Carolina's Francis Marion National Forest were no match for Hurricane Hugo. The fallen trees were later salvaged by loggers. (Bottom) Boat owners in Dartmouth, Massachusetts, survey the damage done by Hurricane Bob.

(Top) The landmark water tower was one of the few structures left standing in this section of Florida City, one of the communitities hardest hit by Hurricane Andrew. (Bottom) Hurricane Andrew, with wind speeds peaking at 164 mph (264 kmph), flattened and flooded homes, leaving parts of Dade County, Florida, with little more than mangled lumber, metal, and glass.

cracks in windows, walls, and doors.

Along the coast, the storm surge drags tons of water onto the shore. The sea level may rise as much as 20 feet (6 m), pushing water further onto land. On top of the surge, huge waves 5 to 10 feet (1.5–3 m) high crash over anything in their path. The force of the water erodes beaches and washes away roads and bridges. Small buildings crumble beneath the weight and force of the water.

In areas where a well-defined eye passes directly overhead, the violent storm is interrupted by a period of relative calm. Inside the eye, the air is hot and muggy. The pressure is so low that people can feel it in their ears. About twenty or thirty minutes later, the wind suddenly slams ashore from the back side of the storm. This time it blows from the opposite direction. It may be several more hours before the storm finally passes on.

Towering hurricane waves flood streets, erode beaches, weaken bridges and roadways, and smash structures too weak to withstand their awesome force.

A tropical cyclone over the Bay of Bengal in 1991 caused severe flooding in the tiny country of Bangladesh. More than 100,000 people died as a result of the storm.

Not all the wind damage comes from the hurricane winds. Some hurricanes spawn tornadoes. Although these tornadoes are generally milder than other forms of the twisters, they can contribute to the amount of damage associated with the storm.

DEATH OF A HURRICANE

A hurricane weakens and dies when it is cut off from its fuel of warm water from the ocean. This happens when it moves into cooler water or when it travels over a large land mass. The friction caused by the storm dragging across the land also contributes to its decay.

Even a dying hurricane is dangerous. While traveling across the ocean, the hurricane picks up tons of water each day. The dying storm releases this water, causing some of the world's heaviest rainfalls. The resulting floods have caused great damage and loss of life.

PREPARING FOR A HURRICANE

It is foolish to think that a hurricane will not hit a particular coastline just because one has never been there before. Anyone living along the Atlantic or Gulf coasts of the United States should realize that the possibility exists that a hurricane may hit their area sometime. Being well prepared is the key to saving lives and cutting down on property damage.

Store owners in New York City hope tape will keep Hurricane Gloria from shattering their windows.

Workers in New Orleans rush to board up windows to minimize the damage from Hurricane Andrew.

You should know the elevation of your home above sea level, the location of the nearest evacuation shelter, and the best escape route from your area. High winds easily blow out windows, so you should have shutters or lumber available to board up windows. Your family should also have a storm emergency kit that includes fresh batteries, flashlights, a portable radio, canned foods, and other supplies which you might need when a storm hits.

WHEN A HURRICANE WATCH IS ISSUED

A hurricane watch means that hurricane conditions could possibly hit your area within the next twenty-four to thirty-six hours.

Fill the car with gas. During an evacuation many stations run out of gas. Also, if the electricity goes off, gas pumps won't work.

Stock up on foods that do not need cooking or refrigeration. Have clean, air-tight containers ready to store enough drinking water to last several days. Also, make sure you have enough first aid supplies and medications.

If you have a boat, secure it tightly or move it to a safe place.

WHEN A HURRICANE WARNING IS ISSUED

A warning means that there is a good chance a hurricane will hit your area in less than twenty-four hours. Now is the time to act.

If you live on a coastline, offshore island, near a river or in a flood plain, plan to leave immediately for a safer location. Mobile homes should be evacuated unless they are far inland. Don't wait until the last minute to leave. Low lying areas can flood long before the main part of the hurricane arrives. Roads and bridges may be closed or jammed with others trying to evacuate.

Keep listening to radio or television for updates on the progress of the storm.

Board up windows. Outdoor objects that might be blown away must be anchored or stored inside.

Water is often contaminated during a hurricane. Fill containers, even the bathtub, with several days' supply of

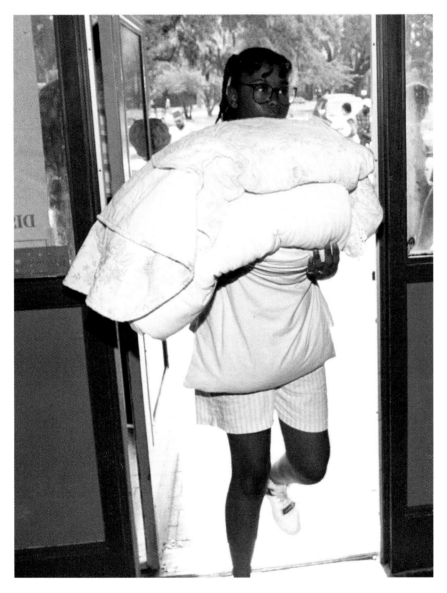

A resident of Charleston, South Carolina, moves into an emergency evacuation shelter to safely wait out Hurricane Hugo.

fresh drinking water.

Turn refrigerators and freezers to their coldest settings and don't open them unless necessary. This will cut down on food spoilage if the electricity goes off.

Remain at home if your house is sturdy and on high ground. Stay indoors in the middle of the house, away from windows and glass doors. Bring pets inside.

Don't go outside into the eye of the hurricane. The violent eye wall may hit before you can get back safely.

AFTER THE STORM

Seek medical help if necessary at Red Cross disaster stations or hospitals.

Be careful going out after a hurricane. Streets may be filled with broken glass and other dangerous debris. Loose and dangling power lines can electrocute anyone who touches them. Roads and bridges may be weakened and could collapse. Floods may bring poisonous snakes and insects out of hiding.

Stay away from river banks and streams until all threat of flooding has passed.

4

FORECASTING HURRICANES

EARLY FORECASTING

Long ago, people didn't know a hurricane was coming until it was too late to get out of the way. As a result, hurricanes were responsible for thousands of deaths.

Father Benito Viñes, a priest living in Cuba, was the first person to devote his life to studying hurricanes. Using his own daily weather observations and reports from steamship captains and volunteers, Father Viñes tracked hurricanes in the area. His first prediction was on September 11, 1875, two days before a hurricane ravaged parts of Cuba. His warnings gave people time to prepare. Because of his work, Father Viñes earned the nickname of "The Hurricane Priest."

During World War II, radar was used to detect enemy ships and aircraft from great distances. As a bonus, scientists discovered that it could also detect storms. Today, radar is used to track hurricanes and typhoons when they are within a couple hundred miles of land. Radar has improved since World War II. Today's Doppler radar can detect the movement of raindrops and other objects within the storm clouds. From this, meteorologists can determine the speed and direction of the wind inside a storm.

HURRICANE HUNTERS

In 1943, a spur-of-the-moment experiment by a daring pilot in the Army Air Corps provided a new way of looking at hurricanes from the inside. Colonel Joseph Duckworth and his navigator flew their single engine plane through the raging wall of storm clouds into the eye of a hurricane threatening the Texas coast. His flight was such a success that aircraft reconnaissance became an important part of hurricane forecasting.

Today "hurricane hunters" or "storm trackers" fly planes loaded with meteorological instruments into the heart of approaching storms. Dropsondes, which are canisters containing weather instruments, are dropped into the eye. As each dropsonde floats down to the sea carried by a parachute, it records information on temperature, pressure, wind direction, and humidity. The information is transmitted to computers aboard the plane, then sent to computers at the National Hurricane Center. This allows meteorologists to continually analyze the storm.

Some meteorologists believe that aircraft reconnaissance is unnecessary. They feel the information they need can be gathered from satellites and other safer methods. Flights into typhoons in the Pacific Ocean have already been discontinued. But most people at the National Hurricane Center feel that both satellite and reconnaissance data are needed. They feel that these flights provide information that can't be found by other means. For example, hurricane hunters are likely to be the first to track the rapid strengthening that often occurs as hurricanes approach land.

Perhaps someday satellites and other methods of

A gas-filled balloon carries weather instruments aloft to collect information about current conditions in the atmosphere.

studying hurricanes will be capable of providing the information aircraft reconnaissance now provides, but until then, hurricane hunters are likely to remain an important part of hurricane forecasting.

SATELLITES

Ever since the first weather satellite, TIROS, was launched in 1960, satellites have been an important tool in gathering information about the earth's weather.

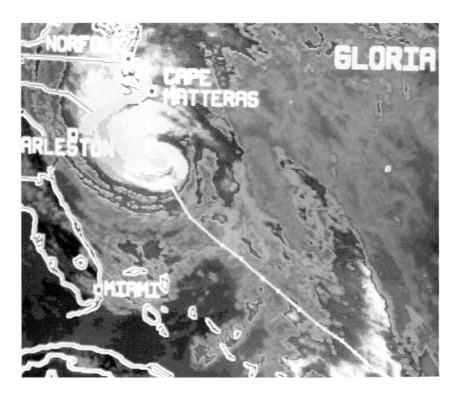

A color-enhanced satellite photo shows Hurricane Gloria moving toward the coast of North and South Carolina.

From hundreds of miles above the Earth, a satellite photographs the heavy mass of clouds swirling around the eye of Hurricane Elena.

There are two basic types of weather satellites. Polar-orbiting satellites circle the earth every 100 minutes or so. From their orbit 400 to 600 miles (640 to 965 km) above the earth, they send back a steady stream of information about our planet and its atmosphere.

Other satellites travel in a geostationary orbit 22,000 miles (35,400 km) above the equator. Because they travel at the same speed as the Earth rotates, they are always above the same spot.

Weather satellites give meteorologists their first look at the heavy, spiralling clouds that may develop into a hurricane. The satellites also show weather systems near a hurricane that might influence its strength or path. Satellite information can also be used to estimate the strength of hurricanes.

COMPUTERS

Computers help meteorologists study hurricanes in two ways. First, computers receive enormous amounts of weather data collected from satellites, radar, airplanes, weather balloons, ground stations, and other sources. High-speed computers digest the data and print out the information for meteorologists to use in making their forecasts.

Computers can also recreate pictures of hurricanes. These pictures are called computer models. Instead of studying an actual storm, scientists can study computer models to learn how hurricanes develop and behave. These models can also be used to help predict where a particular hurricane will make landfall.

Predicting where a hurricane will hit land can be tricky. Hurricanes can go straight, zigzag, or even loop. This makes it very difficult to forecast where some storms will go. If forecasters issue a warning to an area that is too small, they might miss the actual landfall location. If they warn an area that is too large, a lot of money could be wasted on

Meteorologists at the National Hurricane Center in Coral Gables, Florida, use computers to track hurricanes and learn more about their behavior.

Dr. Bob Sheets, director of the National Hurricane Center, plots the path of old storms as a part of a project to improve the center's forecasting ability.

unnecessary preparations. Scientists are continually studying hurricanes, trying to learn more about their formation, life cycle, and movement.

In the United States, the organization primarily responsible for hurricane tracking and forecasting is the National Hurricane Center (NHC) in Coral Gables, Florida. It is part of the National Weather Service, which is part of the National Oceanic and Atmospheric Administration (NOAA). People at the NHC keep a watchful eye on the tropics, especially during hurricane season. When a storm develops, they track it with satellites, aircraft, radar and other equipment. (Hurricane Andrew struck the NHC itself, toppling its satellite dish, but they made rapid repairs and were back in action within hours of Andrew's landfall.)

The NHC issues a *hurricane watch* when there is a threat of hurricane conditions within twenty-four to thirty-six hours. Those in the affected area should listen for advisories and be prepared to act quickly if necessary.

If a hurricane is expected to reach an area within twenty-four hours or less, a *hurricane warning* is posted. This is a call for immediate action.

PROJECT STORMFURY

Attempts have been made to tame the awesome forces of hurricanes. The most elaborate attempt was Project Stormfury, an experimental program funded by NOAA. Scientists hoped the project would produce a way to reduce hurricane winds. These scientists had observed that a tighter eye wall produced stronger winds. They hoped to find a way to widen the eye, which in turn might reduce the winds.

During Project Stormfury clouds in the eye wall were seeded with silver iodide to cause more rain to fall. This caused more heat to be released. Scientist hoped this would cause the eye wall to move outward.

Between 1961 and 1971, four hurricanes were seeded. Three of them showed some reduction in wind speeds, but the fourth showed no such change. Later, in some hurricanes that were not seeded, the eye wall moved outward on its own. Because of this, the scientists could not prove that the seeding had worked at all. Experiments with seeding hurricanes ended in 1972 with no clear conclusions.

Tampering with nature could do more harm than good. Controlling hurricanes in one place might keep another part of the world from getting the rain it desperately needs.

5

SCIENCE PROJECTS AND RELATED ACTIVITIES

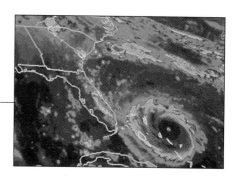

The following are some activities you may do at home or at school to learn more about hurricanes and the atmosphere they develop in.

Air Pressure. The air pressure around us is much stronger than we might realize. You can see air pressure at work with the following experiment. You will need a thin wooden ruler and three large sheets of newspaper.

Place the ruler so that about one-third of it is over the edge of a table. Place the sheets of newspaper over the ruler and smooth them down. With a quick blow, hit the ruler to see if you can make the newspapers fly up in the air. What happened?

It is quite possible that your ruler broke or at least didn't move. The air pressing down on the large sheets of newspaper supplied enough weight to keep the paper and ruler from moving.

Light and Heavy Air. Storms such as hurricanes would not be possible if warm air didn't rise. This rising air carries moist air to a height where it condenses to form clouds. You

The weight of the air pressing down on the surface of this newpaper is enough to keep a ruler from moving when hit.

can see that warm air rises with the following experiment. You will need a glass bottle, a balloon and a rubber band.

Cool the bottle in the refrigerator for fifteen minutes or so. Fasten a deflated balloon tightly over the mouth of the bottle and let it stand. What happens when the air inside the bottle warms? You can obtain faster results by warming the bottle under hot running water. As the air warms, it expands and rises into the balloon.

You can also reverse this experiment. Warm a bottle in hot water. Fasten a deflated balloon over the top and put the bottle in the refrigerator. As the air cools, it sinks, pulling the balloon down with it.

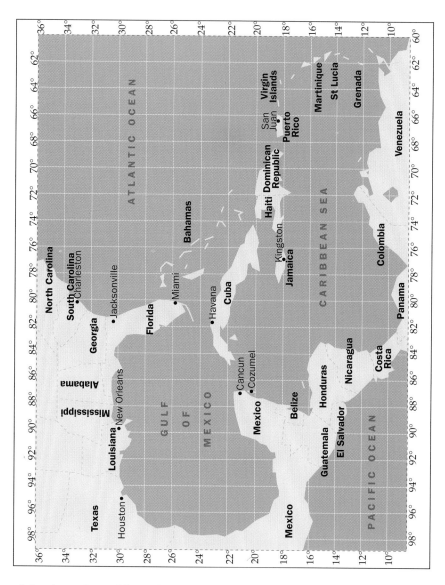

A hurricane's position, given in latitude and longitude, is updated every six hours. The storm's path can be determined by marking these coordinates on a hurricane tracking map.

Weather Forecasting. Save the weather maps from the newspaper for one week. Find high and low pressure areas and see what kind of weather cities in those areas are experiencing. Watch the high and low pressure areas for the next several days. Do they move? In which direction? How does the weather change in those areas? Predict tomorrow's weather for your city or for some other city on your weather map. Check the paper tomorrow to see if you were right.

Tracking a Hurricane. Meteorologists report the location of a storm's center by giving its coordinates. A coordinate is a geographic point measured in terms of latitude and longitude. Latitude lines are those running east and west (normally across the map). Longitude lines are those running north and south (normally up and down the map). If a meteorologist reports that a hurricane is at latitude 25° north and longitude 90° west, you would find those two lines on the map and put a dot where they intersect.

Using the hurricane tracking map on the opposite page, find where a hurricane would be if its coordinates were (1) 25° north and 85° west, (2) 30° north and 80° west, (3) 23° north and 82° west.

What are the coordinates for (1) Miami, Florida, (2) Havana, Cuba, and (3) New Orleans, Louisiana?

The next time there is a tropical storm or hurricane, listen to weather reports on radio or television and mark the coordinates on your map. By listening to the updated coordinates every six hours, you can track the path of the storm.

Much of the damage to homes and other structures could be reduced if they were built using hurricane-resistant features.

Science Reports. The following topics will help you learn more about hurricanes, weather, and weather forecasting. One of them may make an interesting topic for a science report or for doing research on your own.

Computer Models
Coriolis Force
Disaster Relief
Hurricane Andrew
Hurricane Hunters
National Hurricane Center
Project Stormfury
Radar
Saffir-Simpson Scale
Storm Surges
Weather Satellites
Wind

Book Reports. Going through a hurricane can be terrifying. The characters in the following stories learned a great deal through their experiences in contending with these monstrous storms.

Epstein, Sam & Beryl. *Hurricane Guest.* New York: Random House, 1964.

McNulty, Faith. *Hurricane.* New York: Harper & Row, 1983.

Rumsey, Marian. *Carolina Hurricane.* New York: Morrow, 1977.

Winthrop, Elizabeth. *Belinda's Hurricane.* New York: Dutton, 1984.

GLOSSARY

aneroid barometer — Measures air pressure by reading the strength of the air pressing against a metal chamber from which part of the air has been removed. As the chamber expands and contracts, a dial indicates the air pressure measurement.

barometer — A device used to measure air pressure. Two types of barometers are the mercury barometer and the aneroid barometer.

barometric pressure — Air pressure, called barometric pressure because it is measured with a barometer.

Coriolis force — A force resulting from the earth's rotation that causes winds in low pressure systems to curve counterclockwise in the Northern Hemisphere, and clockwise in the Southern Hemisphere.

cyclone — A storm or system of winds that rotates around a center of low pressure.

eye — The center of a hurricane, where winds are relatively calm, air pressure is lowest, and the air is warmest.

eye wall — The bank of violent thunderstorms that surround the calm hurricane eye; contains the hurricane's most damaging winds and heaviest rain.

hurricane warning — The advisory issued by the National Hurricane Center when there is a good chance that hurricane conditions will occur within twenty-four hours.

hurricane watch — The advisory issued by the National Hurricane Center when there is a possible threat of hurricane conditions within twenty-four to thirty-six hours.

mercury barometer — A device consisting of mercury in a container; air pressure forces the mercury up a tube, and the height the mercury reaches is the air pressure measurement.

outflow shield — The canopy of clouds formed by warm air rising up and out of a hurricane.

rainbands — Long strips of clouds spiraling toward the center of a hurricane that may stretch as far as several hundred miles from the hurricane itself.

Saffir-Simpson Scale — The scale by which hurricanes are ranked according to intensity.

storm surge — The mound of water that accompanies a hurricane as it hits land, raising the sea level by as much as 20 feet (6 m).

tropical depression — Develops out of a tropical disturbance; a mass of thunderstorms with wind speeds of less than 38 mph (61kph).

tropical disturbance — A large area of thunderstorms developing out of a tropical wave.

tropical storm — Develops out of a tropical depression; a mass of thunderstorms with winds from 39–74 mph (63–118 kmph).

tropical wave — A mass of showers and thunderstorms that travels over tropical waters, picking up warm, moist tropical air; it can develop into a tropical disturbance, and, eventually, a hurricane.

FOR FURTHER READING

Books

Alth, Max and Charlotte. *Disastrous Hurricanes and Tornadoes.* New York: Franklin Watts, 1981.

Ellis, Michael J. *Hurricane Almanac.* Corpus Christi, Texas: Hurricane Publications, 1987.

Erickson, Jon. *Violent Storms.* Blue Ridge, PA: Tab Books, 1988.

Lee, Sally. *Predicting Violent Storms.* New York: Franklin Watts, 1989.

Parker, Sybil P. (ed.). *McGraw Hill Encyclopedia of Ocean and Atmospheric Sciences.* New York: McGraw Hill, 1980.

Ruffner, James A. and Frank E. Bair (eds.). *The Weather Almanac.* Detroit: Gale Research, 1984.

Tufty, Barbara. *1001 Questions Answered about Hurricanes, Tornadoes & Other Natural Air Disasters.* New York: Dover Publications, 1987.

Magazine Articles

Brandli, Hank. "Hurricane Hunters." *Popular Mechanics.*
September
1989, p. 68.

DeAngelis, Dick. "The Hurricane Priest." *Weatherwise.*
October
1989, p. 256.

Pampe, William R. "A Hurricane!" *Science and Children.*
September
1986, pp. 16 19.

Pamphlets

Pamphlets and brochures are available from the following organizations:

National Oceanic and Atmospheric Administration,
Rockville, MD 200852.

Insurance Information Institute, 110 William St.,
New York, NY 10038.

INDEX

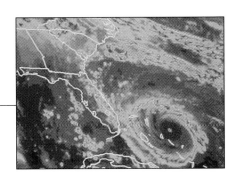

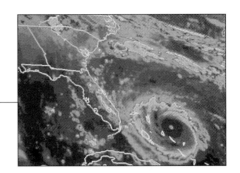

ABOUT THE AUTHOR

Sally Lee is a former special education teacher who has written five other books for Franklin Watts including *Donor Banks, Predicting Violent Storms,* and *The Throwaway Society.* She lives in Sugar Land, Texas with her husband, Steve, a petroleum engineer, and her two children, Mike and Tracy.